How to Create
An Independent
Reading Program

by Leo Schell

SCHOLASTIC
PROFESSIONAL BOOKS

New York • Toronto • London • Auckland • Sydney

The first one was for Joy and so is this one—
as is appropriate.

Special thanks to Rebecca McMillin, Tina
Seymour, and Muriel Woods.

Design direction by Vincent Ceci.
Cover illustration by Mona Mark.
Text design by Kate Panzer.

ISBN 0-590-49135-0

12 11 10 9 8 7 6 5 4 3 2 1   1 2 3 4 5/9

Printed in the U.S.A.

Table of Contents

Preface

Independent reading is an essential component of a balanced elementary-school reading curriculum. It best meets its objectives when it is planned, organized, systematic, sound, stimulating, and varied—when it is a *program*. Teachers need to be able to handle such a large undertaking efficiently, quickly, and with a minimum of effort. These are the goals of this book.

The suggestions in this book come from several hundred elementary-school teachers—mostly in Kansas but some in numerous other states—who contributed ideas on "tried and tested, practical, realistic, feasible ways to get students excited about and interested in reading non-basal readers." These teachers are the true authors of this book.

The suggestions are mostly those that an individual teacher could implement, because most teachers—particularly new ones—tend to operate independently more often than they cooperate with teachers and other professionals. However, any of the suggestions could be expanded to include two or more classrooms or teachers. There is also a section titled "Cooperative Celebrations" that discusses multiple-teacher possibilities such as book fairs and sleep-overs.

There is no guarantee that just because one teacher suggested an idea it will work for another teacher. User discretion is necessary. Also, because many suggestions are written in capsule form, a prospective user will need to do some planning before implementing them. These suggestions are more like a recipe that has to be blended and cooked than like "heat-and-serve" food.

The suggestions should be read with an open mind. An idea shouldn't be rejected simply because "it's not appropriate for my students." Many suggestions can be modified or adapted and made to be quite successful.

Last, the suggestions are not exhaustive. Your favorite idea may not be included. But the ones that are included should permit busy teachers to have a better program on independent reading for all of their students.

A possible problem with this handbook is that it may unintentionally convey the impression that a quality independent reading program may be an overwhelming task— even for an experienced teacher—and a near-impossible one for an inexperienced teacher. It would be erroneous to draw this conclusion. The book was written to help, not to hinder; to inspire, not to discourage; and to simplify the task, not to make it more difficult.

Introduction

Larry Bird didn't become a world-class basketball player merely by playing during scheduled practices and games. He practiced regularly during the off-season, even on Saturdays and Sundays, got to the gym before all of the other players and shot baskets while they were still in the locker room, and stayed to practice some more after the others had departed. Is there a moral here for teachers wanting to produce world-class readers?

Two prerequisites for optimal reading growth are quality instruction and adequate independent reading. Most schools and teachers provide satisfactorily for the former through specified reading lessons, direct teacher instruction, and commercial and teacher-made material. But a quality independent-reading program requires more than a weekly trip to the school library followed by ten minutes of silent reading of checked-out materials. It requires three elements: a variety of appropriate materials, a commitment by the teacher, and a wealth of ideas on how to interest and motivate.

The first two of these elements are the easiest to meet. Most school libraries have an adequate supply of appropriate books, magazines, and even filmstrips and videotapes. And nearly all teachers can make the necessary commitment. This book focuses on the third element: practical classroom-tested suggestions to arouse and sustain student interest in and motivation for independent reading.

An independent reading program is necessary no matter what kind of an instructional program the teacher uses: basal-reader, literature-based, individualized, whole-language, or an eclectic combination of these supplemented by computers. Instructional programs teach students how to read, and they provide practice in reading. Typically they are teacher-selected and teacher-directed. As such, they are structured and organized, usually with assignments and even some kind of teacher evaluation. However, true independent programs are just the opposite. They stress self-selection and self-pacing, are for enjoyment and personal pleasure rather than instruction and learning, and typically aren't teacher-evaluated. Independent reading permits students to explore a variety of print materials for their own purposes without being evaluated on how well or how fast they do it. Freedom and choice are hallmarks of true independent reading programs.

However, independent reading supplements the instructional reading program and helps attain many of the same worthy educational goals that the instructional program is designed to meet. A few of these objectives are:

1. Continued growth in reading skills

2. Exposure to a variety of reading materials

3. A deepening interest in and commitment to reading, printed material, and the reading act

4. An enlarging and deepening of knowledge and information

5. A deeper understanding of how print information is organized and communicated

6. Stimulation of imagination and mental imagery

7. A better understanding of and empathy for others

8. A more profound understanding of self

9. Establishment of personal goals and ambitions

10. A heightening of the desire to write for others to read

As with any worthwhile curricular area, independent reading best attains these objectives when it is a *program*— that is, if it is planned, organized, systematic, and varied. Spur-of-the-moment decisions and hastily implemented ideas will not be as successful, satisfying, or sound as those that are thoughtfully conceived and executed. Hence, this book encourages a program of independent reading rather than a set of uncoordinated hit-and-miss activities. The final chapter, "Teacher-Suggested Guidelines for Creating a Program," expands this idea and even provides a form to facilitate such planning. Teachers shouldn't be reluctant to plan, organize, and implement such a program; the dividends far exceed the effort.

One of the delights of implementing an independent reading program is that it can be a creative venture filled with stimulating, imaginative activities. There are no behavioral objectives for the independent reading program, no mandated tests to measure achievement, no worksheets that must be evaluated and recorded, and no teacher's manual to be followed step-by-step. Rather, because the goals of independent reading are student pleasure, delight, and satisfaction, teachers can be freer, more original, and more inventive than they can be in the instructional program. Independent-reading programs provide satisfactions for both teachers and students that instructional programs can't.

An independent reading program contributes to nearly all aspects of human growth and development. Children become more human, more civilized, and more mature as they read independently. A program of independent reading isn't just an educational nicety; it's an educational necessity. In the poem on the next page, Nancy Whitelaw has memorably and delightfully expressed the values of and the necessity for such a program.

SOME NEGATIVE AND POSITIVE THOUGHTS
ON READING IN SCHOOL

Nancy Whitelaw

Having a reading program based on just
diagnosis and prescription is like making a cake
and not tasting it—
    Like notes of music on paper—
    Like a library with closed doors—
    Like a marriage by contract.

Reading without sharing is like watching
a circus without saying anything—
    Like a commercial without a TV program—
    Like describing a spiral staircase
    without using your hands.

Explaining the rules for determining
whether g is "hard" or "soft" is like
outlining how to play jazz—
    Like measuring a laugh—
    Like measuring an idea—
    Like weighing happiness.

Reading is not a Forty-Five-Minute Period
of Instruction with Behavioral Objectives
and Predictable Outcomes.

Reading is enjoying, learning, feeling, becoming,
sensing, laughing, crying, hating, deciding,
loving, growing, sympathizing, listening.
    Reading is ALL Day—
    Being and Becoming—
    Growing and Growing.

Reprinted with permission of the International Reading Association

The Foundation Of a Quality Independent Reading Program

Quality reading instruction is the foundation of a program of independent reading. The inability to read easily and fluently stifles the will to read. Five aspects of the instructional program are paramount:

1. Match student and book in reading instruction. In reading instruction, students should read materials at their Instructional or Independent reading levels, not any more difficult. Authorities generally agree on the following criteria for identifying these levels:

PERCENT OF ACCURACY			
Level	Word Recognition	Comprehension	Other Evidence
Frustration	Below 95%	Below 70%	Copy oral reading;signs of anxiety and tension—e.g. squirming
Instructional	95-98%	75-90%	Mostly fluent reading;few signs of difficulty—e.g. hair twisting
Independent	98%	90%	Rhythmic, expressive oral reading. No observable symptoms or difficulty —e.g. finger pointing

Day after day of attempting to read too-difficult material will inevitably create a negative attitude toward reading that will overshadow any positive effects the independent reading program may have. Therefore, no matter what positive and stimulating activities a teacher implements, the effects will be slight or nonexistent if—during reading instruction—students are assigned to read materials that are too difficult.

Most textbooks on reading instruction and even many basal-reader teacher manuals provide specific information on how to determine a student's reading level. Additionally, many basal-reading series have informal reading inventories that can be used for this purpose. And Chapter 1 teachers and teachers of learning-disabled students have copies of such instruments.

Many authorities on remedial reading believe that beginning readers who are struggling to learn to read should be given material at the Independent level where they make few errors. They cite research indicating that these young children make better progress using materials at their Independent level. For these children, the Instructional level can become the Frustration level.

2. Teach skills that permit independence and success. If, in independent reading, students don't recognize words, don't have the ability to pronounce unrecognized words, fail to determine the meaning of words not in their vocabulary, or are unable to work out the meaning of what they read, they will not enjoy reading on their own and will avoid it.

Even though this implies well-taught skill lessons, research indicates some teachers overemphasize skills instruction and assign students more worksheets than are necessary for satisfactory learning. In such situations, students can come to equate reading instruction with completing worksheets rather than understanding, learning, and pleasure. The role of skill instruction must be kept in perspective.

3. Use a variety of instructional materials. A few teachers and school districts have mistakenly concluded that a single basal reader constitutes a total instructional reading program and that these materials are to be used daily. Students find even the best basal-reading materials monotonous, tedious, and unappealing if they are used daily throughout the year. Various instructional materials should be used at regular intervals to avoid ennui and apathy. A form in the final chapter of this book should help you produce variety.

4. Vary grouping patterns. Many reading authorities recommend grouping for reading instruction, and many teachers find this a desirable practice. But being in the same reading group day after day—especially if the same book is used—can quickly turn even the most avid reader into an apathetic one. There are numerous organizational patterns, most described in reading-instruction textbooks. Using a different pattern one day a week, for several consecutive days, or even for several weeks at a time energizes students and helps keep attitudes toward reading instruction positive.

5. Use student oral reading judiciously, discreetly, and purposefully. Many teachers, particularly in the primary grades, have students do a lot of oral reading of instructional material. This is a justifiable practice for many reasons that nevertheless can be overdone, particularly when it degenerates into "round-robin" or "barbershop" reading ("Next, please"). Research has shown that one of the most distasteful things older students remember about elementary-school reading instruction was excessive oral reading. Fortunately, it's easy to avoid excessive oral reading.

If these five principles are followed, the groundwork for a quality program of independent reading will have been laid, thereby helping to assure its success.

Creating an Environment Conducive to Reading

A warm, print-filled, nonthreatening environment simplifies the teacher's job. It repeatedly says to students, "Let's read; reading is fun and satisfying." The message is so clear and compelling that few students can resist its lure. First we'll examine sources of printed material for both you and your students, and then we'll describe elements necessary for a physically and psychologically inviting classroom.

Sources of Reading Materials

A satisfactory independent reading program has a variety of materials at different levels available to meet the interests and abilities present in typical classrooms. There are four sources of such materials: the classroom library, the school library/media center, students' homes, and student-written materials.

THE CLASSROOM LIBRARY

A small classroom library is essential to a successful independent reading program because it keeps material constantly available for browsing, stimulation, and reading. Sometimes the library is part of a reading corner, see page 24. Following are some guidelines on operating this library.

1. Familiarize yourself with the materials to determine the variety, interests, reading levels, and correlation with curricular areas—e.g., science, math, and social studies.

2. Provide some way to regularly display a few materials at a time; don't leave them all shelved under the window. When the materials are displayed, briefly comment on them, indicating content, genre, level of reading, and even your opinion of each piece.

3. Formulate a long-range plan for displaying materials. Some suggestions are in the section about the reading corner, on page 24.

4. Formulate use and checkout policies. Determine whether materials are for in-room use only, whether they can be taken home, and how long they can be checked out. Decide whether students can check materials out independently, should consult a room librarian, or should go through you. (Some teachers establish rules and procedures with their students.)

5. At the beginning of the school year, take an interest survey of your class to determine their reading tastes. Use this information to expand the classroom library.

6. Spend some time the first few days acquainting students with all materials already collected, particularly those not on display.

7. Provide times for students to browse through materials. Establish guidelines for the number of students that can be in the area at the same time, how long they can stay, and how they should return materials.

8. Periodically supplement your classroom library by borrowing from the school library/media center, the public library, or the bookmobile. This will be particularly necessary should you engage in an author or topic study as described on pages 59-60.

9. Many teachers build their classroom libraries by using paperback-book clubs. These clubs send monthly catalogs of available books. Some teachers use school discretionary money to buy these books to supplement classroom libraries. The book clubs also offer free copies for every so many books ordered by students, and some teachers add these copies to their classroom libraries.

10. If the classroom library is meager, sometimes there is school discretionary money available to buy books and magazines. Used-book stores and garage sales can be a source of inexpensive materials—thereby stretching a slim budget. Some teachers have appealed to parents for used books from their children's collections and have received hardbacks, paperbacks, and magazines. Teachers can add free or inexpensive materials such as catalogs, which are quite appealing to students. And school librarians will sometimes donate outdated but nevertheless appealing magazines.

THE SCHOOL LIBRARY/MEDIA CENTER
The independent reading program and the library media center so complement each other that it is hard to think about one without the other. Many school libraries contain not only a wonderfully varied collection of appropriate and appealing books and magazines but also a variety of audiovisual materials, sometimes including videotapes and computer software. A knowledgeable librarian and an enterprising teacher can locate something for even the most difficult-to-reach student to read.

And the library media specialist can be a teacher's best friend in conducting an organized and stimulating independent reading program. Not only do library media specialists intimately know the material in the library media center, but they perform numerous functions such as telling stories, giving book talks, reading poems, helping with creative dramatics, and performing puppet shows—all of which help instill the desire to read. Teachers—particularly inexperienced ones or ones new to a building—should take advantage of the wealth of resources in the library media center. If you are a new teacher or if you have a new library media specialist, here are some tips.

1. Introduce yourself to the library media specialist and find out whether there will be an orientation for new teachers or when you may individually schedule such a session.

2. Find out whether the library media specialist offers scheduled weekly lessons for your students or whether the library media center has a curriculum-integrated program with flexible scheduling. If the former, ask about the content of the lessons and how you may cooperate to maximize their goals.

3. Ask about materials in the library media center and where they are located. Better-equipped library media centers contain not only the traditional books and magazines but also audiovisual materials such as filmstrips, videotapes, records, audiotapes, flat pictures, models, and computer software. Only your imagination limits how they can be used in the independent reading program.

4. Find out about services offered, including the following:
a) Assistance by the library media specialist in locating and gathering materials for lessons/units
b) Lessons for students—e.g., using the card catalog, book talks, special books (reference books, etc.)
c) Bibliographies for units of study or author studies
d) Interlibrary loans
e) Ordering new material

5. Find out about available equipment such as projectors, audio and video recorders, television monitors, and computers

6. Find out about operating procedures such as:
a) Circulation and checkout procedures
b) Card catalog (some newer ones are computerized and may require an explanation on how to use them)
c) Equipment reservation (so you don't rush in at the last minute requiring a video camera and monitor only to find they're all checked out)

d) Equipment storage

e) Equipment repair and how to report problems

7. Ask about books—both fiction and nonfiction—that your students might be interested in. Ask about books popular with students of your grade level, some titles your students may have read last year, and some titles popular with students a grade or two older than your students. Ask whether you can check out several of these and begin familiarizing yourself with them. Continue familiarizing yourself with books as the library media specialist or your students recommend them.

8. If you're an inexperienced teacher, ask the library media specialist for several suggestions appropriate for beginning teachers at the start of the school year on stimulating students to read independently.

9. Find out how the library media center/library media specialist participates in Book Week (mid-November) and National Library Week (early April). Many times these are schoolwide celebrations. Ask how you can cooperate and be involved.

10. Request that the library media specialist regularly share with you new materials appropriate for your students or your curriculum so you can consider using them in your independent-reading program.

The resources of most school library/media centers and the skills of school librarians are vast and filled with potential for helping create a stimulating independent reading program.

STUDENTS' HOMES

Students' homes are a fertile source of materials for independent reading. Students subscribe to magazines, receive books as gifts, and buy books on their own. These should be welcome supplements to the materials available in the school—even if they must occasionally be monitored. Frequently student materials will be about esoteric, ephemeral topics not found in school libraries—e.g., television heartthrobs, monster cars, rock groups, and cartoon characters. Even though these materials can't constitute a total independent reading program, for some students they can be a start and a bridge toward other reading material.

A meager supply of school materials can be supplemented with books and other printed materials students bring from home for others. If marked, recorded, and not permitted to leave the room, these books can be a valuable supplement because many students have varied personal libraries. A teacher can organize such a program by establishing a schedule whereby several students share their libraries each month.

Parents can be asked to donate magazines after they have read them. This works best if the teacher sends home a list of requested magazines rather than merely issuing a blanket request.

All of these materials can be permanent additions to the classroom or merely on loan.

STUDENT-WRITTEN MATERIALS

Many teachers, at all grade levels, have students write books, stories, poems, and reports that are made available for other students to read. Invariably these are eagerly read by classmates. They can provide a delightful mini-supplement to the classroom or school library. This is discussed in "The Reading-Writing-Reading Connection," pages 68-69.

In the Classroom

Five simple elements can create a classroom environment conducive to independent reading: teacher attitude, teacher actions, displays of reading materials, bulletin boards, posters, and mobiles, and a reading corner.

TEACHER ATTITUDE

Teachers needn't know all the best books, good magazines, appealing filmstrips, or motivational techniques in order to have a quality independent reading program—though it helps.

But such a program is impossible unless the teacher has a positive attitude toward the program. The teacher must display delight in varied reading material, sincere interest in what students are reading—even when that material doesn't meet his or her notions of quality literature—and pleasure in independent reading and its values. Even teachers apathetic or resistant to a strong independent reading program begin to change their attitude as they see how their students react favorably to such a program.

TEACHER ACTIONS

Scheduling time for independent reading and providing varied reading materials are the most obvious, essential teacher actions for a quality program, but there are others, too.

Regular oral reading to students. Teachers need to introduce students to a variety of material: riddles, cartoons, novels, short stories, factual information, poems, catalogs, and more. Too many teachers read only novels all the way through, whereas reading parts of books may be more effective in encouraging independent reading and permit exposure to a far wider range of materials. Teachers can select evocative descriptions, action and humorous episodes, suspenseful scenes, and captivating chapters.

Just as sustained silent reading needs a regularly scheduled time, so does teacher oral reading. This time needs to be viewed as a legitimate part of the total reading curriculum. This means that the amount of time scheduled for other curricular areas (e.g., science or social studies) shouldn't be shortened in order to fit in teacher oral reading. Teachers need to maintain a professionally proportioned curriculum. The only professionally justifiable decision is to decrease the reading-instruction period commensurate with the time allocated to teacher oral reading. Many teachers have determined that they could gain a few minutes daily by decreasing the number of worksheets they assign without jeopardizing students' reading competence if they chose wisely which worksheets to eliminate.

Sharing materials with students. Students have a limited knowledge of reading materials, and merely hearing classmates share what they have read is inadequate to enlarge this knowledge satisfactorily. Teachers should regularly share varied material. Sometimes just holding up a book and saying "This is a mystery adventure for the very brave" is adequate. Sometimes a synopsis is more appropriate, while at other times showing the illustrations or reading a few sentences is best.

There are many sources of materials to share. As classroom library displays are regularly changed, materials being displayed can be shared. Or materials related to author or topic studies can be briefly introduced. (See "Author-Topic Study," pages 59-60.) Materials borrowed from the school library/media center, the public library, or the bookmobile can also be shared before being made available to students. Or materials brought from home by students can be briefly introduced.

Some library media specialists even introduce new materials in classrooms. And some enterprising teachers have had principals, school nurses, and parents comment briefly about materials they believe students would enjoy reading.

Teachers who know their students' reading interests can recommend materials to specific students merely by saying, "Marie, if you liked *Clifford, the Big Red Dog*, I'm sure you'll like *Curious George*, which is also about a pet that repeatedly gets into lots of trouble."

Individual conferences. There is nothing more powerful to provoke student interest in reading independently than for a teacher to say sincerely, "Tell me about what you're reading." Such conferences can be brief, merely a question such as "How do you like this book?" or "Did you make a good choice?" It's best if they're impromptu rather than regular or scheduled, maybe only with selected students—those with few reading interests, those unable to persevere in silent reading, or those with negative attitudes toward reading. Conferences should be casual talks, not a discussion or a series of teacher-asked questions designed to substitute for a book report. They can be conducted in a corner or even a closet or the hall during sustained silent reading time.

DISPLAYS OF READING MATERIALS

Just as stores prominently display goods for sale to promote examination and to tempt impulse buyers, so should teachers display reading materials where students can examine them. Shelved books are seldom inviting; how much have you ever learned from the spine of a book?

Displays can be either varied or unified. Varied displays contain different kinds of material—books, magazines, student-written books, book-and-record sets—at different reading levels about different topics. More unified displays would be about a single topic such as magnetism, a theme such as courage, a genre such as biography, an author, or a series of books. Sometimes a unified display can be related to holidays or notable events, other times to units in curricular areas. Even though unified by one element, these displays can still include varied materials at different reading levels.

Teachers in grade 5 and above should consider periodically including some adult reading material such as newspapers and weekly newsmagazines—without stooping to the tabloids found in supermarket checkout lanes.

A shrewd teacher will involve students in many ways in selecting and setting up these displays. Some teachers rotate groups of students, putting a different group in charge of the display. Others emphasize each student's talents and make cooperative displays.

BULLETIN BOARDS, POSTERS, AND MOBILES

Stores announce and advertise their merchandise in various ways; teachers should do likewise with reading materials. Bulletin boards can be informative and stimulating as well as attractive. They are discussed in more detail on pages 56–59.

There are several sources of posters and mobiles. School-supply stores have a variety of them, as do organizations such

as the American Library Association and The Children's Book
Council. There are ones for holidays, seasons, themes (e.g.,
space exploration), and even authors. The school's central
office or the school librarian will have catalogs you can
consult, and the principal may have some discretionary funds
you could spend on such items. And many of your fellow
teachers will lend theirs to you for a month.

A problem with commercial materials is that they may not
focus on the topic you want to emphasize. This means you
must make your own. Veteran teachers give neophytes the
following advice about making their own bulletin boards,
posters, and mobiles:

1. Don't spend more time making them than they merit.
Quality artistic productions may require more time and effort
than they are worth, time and effort you could spend on more
valuable things.

2. Make materials that you feel sure you can reuse in the future, probably next year. It may be unwise to spend time on something you're going to discard after just two weeks' use.

Experienced teachers relate how they have spent significant time—and in some cases, their own money—to make or buy bulletin boards, posters, or mobiles only to find students virtually ignored them. Teachers need to help students be aware of such projects. Don't just exhibit them and expect students to react positively.

READING CORNER

Many teachers, particularly in the primary grades, find that a reading corner stimulates independent reading. Sometimes an effective corner can be nothing more than a couple of pillows on the floor or a rocking chair. It can be as elaborate as time and money permit.

If a corner of the room is used, partitions or walls can be created to set it apart. It can be decorated with signs and posters and furnished with beanbag chairs, cushions, or a rocking chair. It can even be decorated to correspond to a holiday: black and orange crepe-paper streamers for Halloween; red and white hearts for Valentine's day. However, veteran teachers commonly caution against spending more time and money than is warranted.

Teachers have used decorated refrigerator boxes or bathtubs filled with pillows. Even small tents have been used. One teacher found a throne used in a local play and reserved it daily for specified "Reading Royalty." And some energetic teachers have even built small lofts.

As with instructional materials, variety is helpful. Consider taking up the carpet and putting away the beanbag chairs and cushions for a week or two. You might want to take a class poll asking students what they'd like to have in the corner. When reestablished, its motivational power and aura will be as strong as ever.

No matter what is created or used, the guidelines governing its use should be agreed upon and clear to the whole class.

TO SUM UP

Appealing and interesting materials are the keys to a successful independent reading program. All the rest—teacher oral reading, individual conferences, displays of materials, reading "corners," even teacher enthusiasm—are merely icing on the cake. Keep things in perspective!

Getting Started: The Nuts and Bolts of Sustained Silent Reading

Getting Started

The simplest and possibly the most effective and efficient way to encourage independent reading is simply to provide time during the school day for such reading. This communicates to students that independent reading is so important that time will be reserved for it. This practice is commonly called sustained silent reading—SSR. But before describing how to initiate and operate an SSR program, let's discuss ways to help students better select appropriate material that they want to and can read. This will include determining students' reading interests, assessing students' attitudes toward reading, and helping students independently select appropriate books.

DETERMINING READING INTERESTS

Interest energizes and focuses behavior. Reading is a solitary activity requiring commitment, self-discipline, and perseverance. And sustained silent reading requires sitting still for a period of time, becoming absorbed in self-selected material, paying attention, and being physically passive but mentally active. These demands aren't natural to active, energetic students. Therefore, material in which they are truly interested is a prerequisite.

Award-winning literature may not hold a student's attention if he or she isn't interested in the topic. Therefore, many teachers—particularly near the beginning of the year—try to determine students' general areas of interest and then match students with appropriate material.

The particular inventory on page 28 is designed to be responded to in writing and therefore isn't appropriate for all students. Teachers should modify it to fit their students' ages and capabilities, even administering it orally to individual students if necessary. Also, teachers need to communicate clearly that the purpose of the questionnaire is to help students enjoy independent reading more by choosing material well. Therefore, students need to understand that this isn't a test, that there are no right or wrong answers, and that honesty and insight are essential. If a teacher can create a more casual and informal atmosphere before and during using the inventory, the results will be more accurate and useful.

Teachers should be particularly concerned with the independent reading interests of less able readers. Frequently these students are less enthusiastic about reading than higher-achieving students. Also, they have a far more difficult time selecting appropriate material because they tend to choose material their peers are reading or have read, material at their developmental level rather than their reading level. (More about this appears in "Helping Students Independently Select Appropriate Books" later in this chapter.) If we can match these lower-achieving students with material they are interested in reading, their attitude and behavior are likely to be more appropriate to the demands of SSR than otherwise would be the case.

The sample inventory on page 28 focuses exclusively on reading interests. Many reading-interest questionnaires ask about hobbies, play activities, television viewing, sports, travel, and the like. Just because a child watches a certain television show doesn't mean he or she necessarily wants to read about it. These may be exclusive interests, the former not reflecting the later. If a student is interested in reading about

READING INTEREST INVENTORY

1. Which stories in our reader have you liked?
   a. _____ b. _____

2. What kind of books do you like to read (funny, adventure, animal, fantasy, outdoors, etc.)?
   a. _____ c. _____
   b. _____ d. _____

3. What are two books you've read recently?
   a _____
   b. _____

4. What book(s) would you like to read or have read to you?
   a. _____
   b. _____

5. If you got a book or magazine for a gift, what would you want it to be about? _____

6. What sports or people or places would you like to find out more about? _____

7. Circle what you like to read besides books.
   Magazines   Comic books   Newspapers   Catalogs

8. In magazines, what kind of stories do you like to read?
   a. _____
   b. _____

9. If you could subscribe to a magazine, which one would it be?
   _____

10. Here are five books/stories. (Hold up 5 books.)
    a. Which one would you most like to read or have read to you? _____
    b. Which one would you be least interested in reading or having read to you? _____

N.B. Teachers, use selectively. Not all of these questions are necessary for one child, nor are they appropriate for all age levels.

a certain television show, a sport, or a hobby, this inventory will reveal it.

Teachers and students should interpret the inventory after completing it. Teachers can collect the sheets, note responses of selected students, and then—probably with the help of the library media specialist—try to locate appropriate materials. Students can also interpret their own responses and use this interpretation to help them make wise choices from the classroom library, the school library, or paperback-book clubs from which they order books.

Students' responses can help them think ahead to the specific books or kinds of books they want to select the next time they visit the school library, public library, or bookmobile. They could record their preferences in a small booklet like that shown at right, which they would take with them. If necessary, a knowledgeable adult might help them locate appropriate materials.

ASSESSING STUDENTS' ATTITUDE TOWARD READING

Attitudes toward reading, just like reading interests, help to determine how motivated a student is to read and how much effort he or she will put forth in order to do so. Just as we need to particularly help students with few or no reading interests find personally appealing material so we also need to identify students who have already decided that they don't like reading. Then we must try through wise selection of reading material and related activities to cause their feelings toward reading to become more positive.

The best tool to assess the attitudes of students in grades 1 through 6 is McKenna and Kear's Elementary Reading Attitude Survey (ERAS). This public-domain instrument enables teachers to estimate attitude level efficiently and reliably because it was scientifically constructed and then standardized on a national sample of 18,000 children.

This inventory can be given to an entire class in a matter of minutes (although it currently must be hand-scored). It gives three separate scores: (1) Recreational reading, (2) Academic reading, and (3) Total. Scores can be determined for individual students or the classroom as a whole.

Because this is a standardized (norm referenced) instrument, the directions must be followed explicitly to give valid and reliable scores. And because it is possible for students to fake their responses—to second-guess the teacher and respond as they believe the teacher wants them to respond—questionable results should be substantiated through teacher observations of significant behavior. Examples of indicators include:

- Reads in spare time in classroom.
- Goes to the library voluntarily.
- Talks about books with other students.
- Completes reading assignments promptly.
- Orders books from paperback-book clubs.

Students who are reliably determined to have a negative attitude toward reading should be singled out for help in selecting materials of special appeal and interest to them, and activities that will help their attitude become more positive should be designed for them.

HELPING STUDENTS INDEPENDENTLY SELECT APPROPRIATE BOOKS

Helping students know how to independently select books of appropriate difficulty is quite important, particularly for less able readers who typically choose books too difficult for them to read easily. Frustration and off-task behavior then frequently result. A teacher needs to explain, demonstrate, and have students practice this skill. And they must remind them to use it when they visit the library or bookmobile.

Older students can be taught the "five finger" technique. The student chooses a passage containing about 100 words. (Be careful: words can fool you. It's easy to overestimate and wind up with 200. Therefore, an early task is to teach children how to estimate 100 words.) The student then reads the passage and each time he or she makes an error (e.g., doesn't know the pronunciation or meaning of a word, or stumbles over a word), one finger is curled into the palm. If five or fewer fingers are curled at the end of 100 words, the book is approximately the correct level. (This roughly corresponds to the 95 percent word-accuracy criteria for the Instructional level on an informal reading inventory.) If five fingers are curled in before the end of 100 words, the book may be too difficult.

However, don't forbid a child from trying to read a book that's too difficult. Some children will want so badly to read a too-difficult book that they'll persevere—and triumph. But do make them aware of the amount of effort such a book will probably require.

For younger children, the five-finger technique is too difficult to apply. An easier way is for the teacher to demonstrate via oral reading the difference between the Instructional (or Independent) level and the Frustration level. This demonstration can be followed by a discussion of why one level is appropriate while another is inappropriate, questionable, or too difficult.

Young students should also become aware of the deceptive level of some books. Many picture books have full-page illustrations with only 10 to 30 words per page and thus appear to be easy to read while in reality they are much more difficult and are intended to be read to a child by an adult rather than to be read by a child. You can't judge the reading level of a book by its illustrations.

Many school and public libraries have collections of high-interest, easy-reading books. These are books whose reading levels are lower than the average reading level of students likely to be interested in their contents. Also their plots are often faster-moving than those of traditional books. There are such books all the way from beginning readers through high-school-age novels. And the difference between interest level and reading level can be significant, or only a grade level or so. There are books for students in grades 7 through 12 that are written as low as the second- and third-grade reading level as well as ones for second-grade students reading at a beginning first-grade level. Teachers should locate these books in their school or public library, introduce them to students reading at a below-average level, and encourage these students to select them for their independent reading.

If students select books too difficult to read comfortably, they may not attain the pleasure and satisfaction they otherwise could have. If students choose too-difficult books too frequently, the amount of reading students will do, their self-concept as readers, and their lifelong interest in and attitude toward reading will suffer. And their behavior won't be conducive to the extended personal reading required by sustained silent reading. Regrettably the importance of students independently selecting appropriate-level books is neither discussed in most reading-instruction textbooks nor described in most basal-reader teacher's guides. Yet it's very important to the satisfactory operation of an independent-reading program.

Sustained Silent Reading

Once you have determined your students' reading interests and attitudes about reading, and guided them toward the selection of appropriate and appealing books, you and they are ready for sustained silent reading: SSR.

During SSR—also known as USSR (Uninterrupted Sustained Silent Reading), SQUIRT (Sustained Quiet Uninterrupted Reading Time), DEAR (Drop Everything and Read)—a scheduled amount of time is regularly spent in independent, self-selected reading, by both students and teacher. Some teachers schedule time daily, others two to three times per week. Each student is required to have chosen a book or magazine beforehand so the class may begin reading silently together for five to thirty minutes without interruptions. Teachers are also expected to read during this time; grading assignments or planning lessons is not acceptable. Some teachers may read interesting materials to a group of readers during this time. (See "Interacting with Less Able Readers," page 55.)

SSR is used to promote and enhance reading pleasure. Thus, book reports and summaries are not required. Students are not directed to read for information or to answer questions about their reading but are allowed to read for personal satisfaction.

The single most frequently asked question about SSR is, Where will the time come from? The only reasonable answer is, from the reading instruction period. Formal direct instructional time in reading should be decreased. Independent reading not only meets many of the same objectives as reading instruction (see Preface) but also allows the child to practice and apply learned reading skills and to strategize a variety of real situations. Therefore, shortening formal instructional reading time to permit independent reading is thoroughly justifiable. Otherwise you would be decreasing the time available for other important curricular areas such as math, social studies, science, and health, thereby causing a curricular imbalance. It is professionally unjustifiable to rob Peter to pay Paul. The only reasonable procedure to use when adding SSR is to shorten the reading period commensurate with the time allocated to SSR.

To be successful, an SSR program has to be planned and organized, not implemented hastily or with little thought. And it must be adapted according to the teacher's needs, the age and reading level of the students, and even school policies and schedules. Therefore, what follows is only a generalized description, not a recipe.

Assume that you have created a classroom environment conducive to independent reading, shown students how to independently select appropriate books, and assessed their reading interests and attitudes toward reading. How do you inaugurate a program of sustained silent reading?

1. Determine the best time. At first, short daily SSR periods are best. Try for a generally quiet time during the day and try to assure no interruptions from the public-address system or visitors; post a DO NOT DISTURB sign on the door. Recommended beginning time periods for different grades are:

K–1 ....5 minutes
2....................6 to 7 minutes
3....................10 minutes

This time can be gradually lengthened according to the students' abilities and the time available.

2. Orient students to what SSR is and how it will operate. Heighten their anticipation by emphasizing self-selection and lack of teacher-led discussions, required reports, and evaluation. Students should discuss their responsibilities and expected behaviors during SSR. Sometimes students will find that a selected piece of material is uninteresting, too difficult, or not what they expected and won't want to continue reading it. If they have given the material a fair chance and don't want to continue, let them choose something else; don't insist that they finish whatever they start. As one librarian said, "There are more books in the world than you could ever read. Don't waste time reading one you don't enjoy."

3. Help students select appropriate material. Make sure that each student has at least one appropriate piece of material before the first period.

4. If students haven't previously participated in an independent-reading program, prepare them for what to do when they come to a word they can't pronounce. Some younger students are so accustomed to having a teacher pronounce these words for them that they will be stumped when this assistance isn't available. To prevent students from running to you for assistance every time they meet an unpronounceable word, discuss with them strategies such as skipping the word or thinking what word would make sense. Consider modeling this procedure or demonstrating how skipping a word usually doesn't prevent comprehension or enjoyment.

5. Kindergarten and first-grade teachers need modified programs. Consider these guidelines:

a) Wait several weeks or more into the school year to begin the program, until you have established control and students have established rudimentary independent work habits.

b) Don't wait until students have independent reading skills. Begin by assigning students picture books you've already read aloud to them, ones in which the illustrations adequately tell the story or will absorb the child's interest, or ones that have been read to them at home.

c) Have everybody sit on the floor. Small groups are best.

d) Don't expect young children to be totally silent during this time. Students will impulsively share books with you and their classmates. And many beginning readers have to "mumble-read." Before beginning the program, discuss appropriate and acceptable behavior.

e) Include regular pre- or post-SSR time for self-evaluation. Young children benefit from being reminded of guidelines and from discussing how well they followed guidelines.

f) At first, don't expect that you'll be able to read independently yourself. You may need to move from group to group, child to child, encouraging them to follow guidelines and briefly listening to their sharing.

Sustaining an SSR program over a period of time requires some teacher involvement.

1. Regularly share books with students either by reading them out loud or by introducing them via brief book talks.

2. Provide time for children to share materials they've enjoyed. This sharing can be brief and highly informal.

3. Invite others to participate. Students from another classroom, the principal, and even parents can add spice and variety by periodically reading silently with the class and then briefly sharing their reading.

4. After a significant period of time—four to eight weeks—drop it for a week.

5. Use a variation of SSR such as DEAR, Drop Everything and Read. Every day for a week, at a time unknown to the students, a buzzer rings and whatever activity is under way (except finger-painting!) is halted and students read for an allotted period of time.

All the other activities suggested in this book can be used to maintain and invigorate a program of sustained silent reading. But without time and books, all these activities fall short of their goal.

Building and
Sustaining
The Program

"**G**et out your books; it's time for SSR," if repeated daily, inevitably will cause SSR's motivating power to dwindle to the point where students reach routinely for their books and read without enthusiasm. Teachers need ways other than a continually renewed source of books to sustain student motivation in independent reading and to periodically invigorate the program. This chapter examines specific ways of stimulating and sustaining the program: reading records, student sharing of and creatively reacting to books, and student reporting on books.

READING RECORDS

It is very satisfying and motivating for students to see evidence of their growth and progress; hence the lasting popularity with students and teachers of construction-paper bookworms slowly lengthening to encircle classrooms. The following suggestions are ways of recording student reading. But first a brief discussion of the distinction between *recording* and *reporting* student reading.

A *report* is some kind of formal evidence, typically written or oral, that a student completed a book. It is always an assignment (did you ever know of a student who volunteered to write a book report?) and usually evaluated by the teacher. A *record* is the student's word that he or she has read a book. There is no written synopsis, no oral presentation to the class, no student judgment of the book, no teacher evaluation. The student says he or she has read the book, and the teacher accepts the child's word unless there is good reason to doubt it. Students are never required to record a certain number of books each grading period, as is often required with reports.

The following ideas are all similar—adding evidence such as segments of a bookworm for each book read. Some are more appropriate for older students, some for younger ones. Some are seasonal, others year-round. However, they needn't be limited to books read. They can also record the number of minutes spent reading.

- Bookworms or caterpillar with circles for body
- Monkey with bananas
- Tree with apples or colored leaves
- Haunted house with ghosts
- Turkey with tail feathers
- Horn of plenty with different kinds of fruit
- Christmas tree with decorations
- Kites with tails
- Flowers with petals
- Maybasket with flowers
- Ice-cream cones with dips
- Thermometer with rising mercury
- Clown with balloons
- Leopard with spots
- Bubblegum machine
- Locomotive with cars
- Footprints on walls
- Climbers scaling a mountain
- Cars racing around a track
- Polevaulter clearing a rising bar
- Fish on a stringer
- Swiss cheese with holes
- Spaceship voyage

- Pizza with pepperoni slices
- Runner on football field
- Journey to a selected destination
- Eggs in an Easter basket
- Dachshund with rectangular body segments

Any activity of this kind can be adapted for a whole class or a group. For example, apples signifying books read could be attached to one tree to record whole-class reading or to several trees for groups. These make colorful bulletin boards.

It may be best to have some kind of goal. This could be for the class to read 100 books, for the bookworm to stretch to the library, for students to read 100 hours, or to get the mercury to the top of the thermometer. Because it can be difficult to keep enthusiasm high for a long period of time, the goal should be appropriate to the ages of the students and clearly communicated to them.

Challenges can encourage students to read more. Many teachers have found both intra- and interclass competition motivational.

But a perennial problem with competition is how to reward the winners without discouraging the losers, because there are always far more losers than winners. Don't hastily embark on a competitive project without carefully thinking through the pros and cons. Competitive projects can be superficially attractive but can have serious negative consequences with regard to the ultimate goal of promoting independent reading.

One teacher created teams composed of one good student, one low-achieving student, and two average students. At the end of one month the team that had read the most pages was permitted to plan a party for the whole class. One principal promised to kiss a pig while on the school roof if students read 5,000 books. They did, he did, and everybody loved it! Teachers might consider challenging a class, a group, or individuals.

Many teachers have some kind of recognition or extrinsic reward if and when a goal is attained. Rewards may range from badges to certificates to ice-cream cones to popcorn parties to personal pizzas to paperback books. A simple certificate is shown below. Individuals and groups experience elation and pride in receiving recognition or rewards, and many teachers recommend making the presentation formal and public.

The role of competition and rewards is more complicated—morally, ethically, professionally—than most teachers realize. Many classrooms have charts, publicly posted, like the one below.

ADAM	*	*	*					
BOB	*	*						
CANDY	*	*	*	*	*			
DAWN	*	*						

Such publicly displayed charts are undesirable. They unwittingly encourage competition rather than being records of accomplishments, may reward reading of short or easy books, and become public evidence of who are the less-able readers in the class. The last is particularly undesirable because it may thwart the desire to read by the very students needing most to benefit from independent reading. Perhaps a better solution is to keep private individual records or reading journals rather than public class lists.

If the teacher decides to use some form of competition, number of minutes read may be better evidence than number of books read because one *Little House on the Prairie* may equal 30 *Caps for Sales*. Yet both may be read by second graders in the same classroom who are poles apart in reading achievement.

If the number of books is used, a teacher may need to set differential standards for students by approving books according to students' reading level, reading stamina, and degree of interest in reading. A less-able reader's book may not necessarily be a good-reader's book. Also, because all books are not created equal, a teacher may decide that *Caps for Sale* is "one book" while *Little House on the Prairie* is "20 books."

Rewards need to be thoughtfully weighed and not rashly promised. Not only may they be expensive or require more time than they're worth but some people believe they convey undesirable messages to students: we will bribe you to put forth mental effort and to learn. Reading—and by extension school—could become something done for a tangible reward rather than a worthwhile experience in and of itself; students could start paying more attention to the scoreboard—and the reward—than to the book. Some critics contend that such rewards can debase both children and books.

Even class rewards can present problems. For example, one or two recalcitrant students may prevent the whole class from attaining a goal and its accompanying reward. Or all students may wind up being rewarded whether or not they participated satisfactorily. What will they learn in such instances? "Why should I put forth the effort when I'll be rewarded anyway?"

Contests, competition, and challenges present moral and ethical issues as well as educational ones.

STUDENT SHARING OF AND CREATIVELY REACTING TO BOOKS

The single most potent factor in influencing a student to select a book is a recommendation by another student. Therefore, student sharing must play a central role in an independent reading program. Students can communicate information in two general ways: by sharing and reporting. This section deals with sharing, and the next deals with reporting.

Sharing is somewhat different from reporting. Its purposes include informing classmates about reading material; expressing opinions and views about materials read; and reacting creatively to materials read.

Sharing is usually nongraded, informal, and possibly not required or assigned, whereas reporting may have opposite characteristics. Therefore, sharing and reporting are somewhat contradictory activities. Teachers must thoughtfully decide whether they want students to share, to report, or to do both. Some research has indicated that requiring students to report on a specified number of books each semester or grading period—particularly for a grade—can be counterproductive and inhibit rather than encourage independent reading. On the other hand, such requirements can set academic expectations and provide realistic communication opportunities as well as meet some of the same purposes of sharing listed above. This isn't a decision to be made without considering several variables.

If a teacher decides to have students share—rather than report on—materials read, there are still some crucial decision to be made:

1. How often will sharing time be scheduled?

2. How will it be determined who shares during this time? If it's strictly voluntary, the same extroverted, avid readers

will monopolize sharing time. If not voluntary, then it borders on reporting with the possibility of the attendant negative consequences mentioned above.

3. When will time for creative reaction be scheduled?

4. How much time is appropriate for reacting creatively? How elaborate should sharing be?

Scheduling sharing time at 2:30 every other Friday afternoon won't in and of itself produce quality sharing.

Students love to share satisfying things they have read just as you like to tell your friends about a good movie you've seen. So sharing can be as casual as sitting in a circle with volunteers informally telling about what they have read or as formal as telling the story to classmates via a felt/flannel board.

And students enjoy reacting creatively to a book they've read. It not only permits them to express themselves imaginatively and artistically but causes them to think more deeply about what they have read and to relive parts of it, both educationally worthwhile objectives.

Here are some suggestions for informal sharing:

1. Push back the desks, sit in a circle on the floor, and anyone who wants to—including the teacher—can share a book. Popcorn can be served.

2. A small group of students can eat lunch in the classroom with the teacher and discuss a book all have read or share recently read books. (One teacher called this the Chew and Chat Club.)

3. As early as third or fourth grade, panel discussions are possible. All members may—but need not—have read the same book. Students can discuss problems faced by the main characters, compare solution to problems, describe personality traits of characters, share humorous or suspenseful episodes, or tell why they reacted as they did to the book.

A real advantage of sharing as opposed to reporting is

that the students needn't wait until they have finished reading the book; they can share anytime.

Teacher standards must be appropriate for the students' developmental level. In kindergarten or early first grade, some inexpressive students may merely stand by the teacher's side, hold up a book, and nod their head when the teacher asks, "Did you like the book?" "Did you laugh when you read it?" and "Would you recommend the book to the rest of the class?"

Here are ways students can creatively react to and more formally share what they have read:

- Make a book jacket.
- Draw a scene or character (could be on a transparency).
- Read aloud a good part.
- Give a synopsis (but without revealing the ending).
- Dress as a character.
- Construct a diorama or mural.
- Create a poster.
- Dramatize a scene.
- Make a display of relevant items/props.
- Present a television/radio commercial advertising the book.
- Create a mobile of major characters.
- Make a paper-roll-and-box "movie/television show" by drawing several sequential scenes.
- Make an appropriate bookmark.
- Tell the story using a felt/flannel board.
- Model a clay doll of a major character.
- Use a simple puppet(s) to tell the story.
- Create an appropriate collage.
- Share several reasons others should or should not read the book/material.

- Tell several things learned from the book/material.
- Write a letter to the author giving opinions about the book.
- Record oral presentations on an audiotape recorder and play for the class.
- Videotape presentations and play for class.

Sharing can be as elaborate and inventive as the teacher and students can create—and still be educationally sound. Many of the above suggestions can be expanded or even combined—e.g., a poster may be in the form of a newspaper article complete with headline.

A variation on sharing is to have students rate the books they read. Each time a book is read, the reader rates the book from 1 to 10, 10 being the best. Periodically the ratings are averaged and the order of the books is recorded. A list or poster of the top 10 or 20 books can be displayed in the classroom or library or even shared with the next-youngest grade. The books themselves can be displayed and even honored with a ribbon or certificate.

A "best book" variation is for students to nominate "The Books I'd Take to a Desert Island." Oral explanations can be shared or bulletin boards created. (See the illustration above.)

Because of its potency, student sharing of what they have read deserves a major role in the independent reading program.

REPORTS

Many teachers use some kind of reporting system. This is important when requirements have been set or teacher evaluations or rewards are involved. Reports—oral or written—are legitimate educational activities provided the teacher recognizes their limitations and uses them judiciously.

WRITTEN REPORTS

A standard format for a written report asks for the main character(s), the setting, something about the story, and the student's opinion of the book. Beginning book-report writers can be helped by a form like the one below.

The title is _____

The author is _____

The main characters are _____

_____

Something that I liked was _____

_____

For simple stories with a traditional plot, a macro-cloze format can be used to help students write or orally present reports.

_____
Title

_____
Author

The main characters are _____

_____

First _____

_____

Then, _____

_____

Finally, _____

_____

A more advanced form that also emphasizes story structure is below.

<u>_____</u>
Title

<u>_____</u>
Author

Main characters: _____

The problem they had to solve was_____

_____

To solve it, they _____

_____

The story ends when _____

_____

I rate this book: Poor   Average

Creative teachers can design other forms, too. Characters or the setting could be stressed as well as plot.

An obvious problem with this format is that it isn't appropriate for nonfiction books, biography, poetry, books of riddles and jokes, or even lengthy novels. A nonfiction book report could ask the student to list three facts they learned from the book; a biography book report might ask for summary of one or two main events in the character's life; while a poem or several riddles and jokes could be copied for reports about these kinds of books.

Some teachers have students write the report on a file card that can be referred to by other students looking for an interesting book to read. (Notice rating in above form.)

The "red-pencil syndrome" plagues many teachers reading these reports because they are certain to be laced with misspellings, incorrect syntax, and nonstandard usage. Because independent reading is essentially trying to inculcate a lifetime value system, it's counterproductive for teachers either to grade these reports or to evaluate them for spelling, usage, or syntactical correctness. There are incalculable opportunities when these skills can be legitimately stressed, so it's foolish to crush student self-concept by returning a report graded C or 75 of 100, or liberally decorated with red ink. Evaluation and book reports are antithetical.

Even a small change such as the shape of the paper on which the report is written can make reports seem less onerous. Cut shapes appropriate for the book's topic and make a cover that the student can decorate. Staple the cover and inside sheet together. Here are a few suggestions.

Topic	Shape; cover picture
Baseball	Circle; seams and stitching of a baseball
Detective/mystery	Magnifying glass
Space	Rocket
Cowboys	Ten-gallon hat
Africa	African continent
Treasure hunt	Treasure chest
Ghost story	Ghost

You get the idea. Encourage students to come up with their own ideas based on the book's location, topic, characters, or important objects in the book.

Many teachers combine the independent reading program with the literature program and require students to sample a variety of genres. Individual record charts such as the one below are valuable long-range overviews to direct student reading. When a student has read a book in a category, the title of the book could be written in that space and possibly

CATAGORIES OF BOOKS				
Animals	Mystery/ Adventure	Biography	Non-Fiction	Real Life

even a colorful sticker or seal placed there. Categories should be adapted to the interests of the students.

Teachers who require students to read for a specified amount of time during a grading period have used forms like this one. The number of pages read could be substituted for the number of minutes.

Date	Booktitle	Time Ended	Time Began	Total Time

Name _____   Time _____

Teachers who want to verify reading done outside of school can use a form such as this one. Again, the number of pages could be substituted for the number of minutes.

_____ read for
NAME

_____ minutes.

_____
ADULT

There are several ways teachers have created to give variety to book reports. Some of them follow:

- Write a letter one character might write to another.
- Create a conversation between two or more characters.
- Write a different ending.

- List unusual or colorful words.
- Make a time line.
- Draw a map showing location.
- Compare/contrast two books.
- Write a poem about a character, incident, or plot.
- Write a diary or log that a character might keep.
- Write to the author telling what you enjoyed.
- Prepare questions for a character as if you were a television interviewer.
- Write a letter to a character asking questions about the story.
- Give a demonstration showing how to do something described in the book.
- Make some awards to give characters.
- Write an account of how a character might have acted differently in a situation in the book.
- Draw a picture illustrating the moral of the story.
- Describe a possible sequel.
- Explain why you like (or don't like) the illustrations.
- Tell why you didn't like a character.
- Make a poster with one good quote from the story on it.
- Use reference books to find out more about the author or the illustrator.
- Write several questions or true-false statements for a classmate who has also read the book.
- Write several sentences describing the most outstanding traits of the main character.
- Describe several things in your book that couldn't happen in real life.

Many of the ideas in the section "Student Sharing" could also be used as reports. (See pages 42–45.)

A list of several selected possibilities could be displayed and discussed. Inventive students will even want to add their own possibilities. Possibilities can be added periodically so that by the end of the school year, students will easily find an appealing, nontraditional way to report on their reading.

There are many inexpensive paperbacks of creative book

reports, many with ready-to-duplicate pages. Ask your principal for catalogs of school-supply stores or visit a nearby store.

Even though students react positively to nontraditional book reporting, there are several important decisions teachers have to make. One has to do with when students will have time to create these reports. In school? During SSR or a study period? At home? Will there be standards for these reports or will all submitted work be acceptable? Will finished products be shared orally with you and/or classmates or just turned in? If shared orally with classmates, will this be regularly or whenever a student is ready? Imagine the mess that's possible when ten students are ready to share all at once and you have scheduled time for only two reports. And maybe most important of all, how many book reports will be required during the year and how frequently will they be required?

ORAL REPORTS

Can you recall yourself nervously standing in front of your classmates to give a book report, all of them silently staring at you—or so you thought—and the teacher seated at the desk, grade book in hand? Do you believe students are any different today? Many students find it difficult to give an oral book report. Here are some guidelines for more successful, less stressful reporting.

1. Early in the year, teach students the desired format for oral book reports and model one yourself. Divide into groups and have a student in each group give a prepared report for a story or chapter—not a book—he or she has read or the teacher has read to the class.

2. Show videotapes of "Reading Rainbow" and discuss the book reports students give on the program. "Reading Rainbow" is a delightful 30-minute television program shown mostly in the summer over many noncommercial television stations. Its purpose is to stimulate children to read, and on each show students give oral book reports. School librarians receive information about it. It can be videotaped off the air and shown in classrooms in accordance with copyright laws. Consult your school librarian.

3. Have students hold and show some kind of material— e.g., an illustration in the book, another book by the same author, or any of the products resulting from their creative reaction to the book. Crutches reduce anxiety.

4. Make presentations as informal as possible. Consider a small group of classmates selected by the student gathered away from the rest of the class. Or just to you. If you decide on whole-class presentation, at least have the student who's reporting sit in a chair. Having all students sit on the floor may be even more conducive to relaxed presentations. Questions other students ask of the reporting student may contribute unduly to anxiety.

TO SUM UP

Don't assume that making a book report creative or varied will cause students to respond to it positively. Research has shown that many students dislike—even resent—book reports. This is understandable because such reports essentially, especially if required, say to the student, "I don't trust you; prove to me you read the book." How did you feel about required book reports when you were in school? Do you believe today's students are significantly different from you? Handle book reports—no matter how creative—with the previously listed cautions in mind.

Last, even though nonbook materials are permitted to be read in an independent reading program, there are almost no suggestions on how students can report on these materials. Furthermore, there are no written formats for reports. Teachers who like challenges and consider themselves creative should delight in this situation.

Teacher-Initiated Projects and Activities

Teachers can do more than just provide time and arrange a conducive environment. They can act directly in many ways to stimulate independent reading. In this section, we'll discuss acquainting students with materials, interacting with less able readers, bulletin boards, author/topic studies, reading buddies, home and school, and the reading-writing-reading connection.

ACQUAINTING STUDENTS WITH BOOKS

Students need to be exposed to more reading materials than only the ones their classmates share. There are both formal and informal ways teachers can contribute to this broadening.

Teachers can make students aware of the wide world of available materials for independent reading through brief sharing sessions. The teacher brings an assortment of materials into the room and briefly shares each one—e.g., "This is a book of tall tales; nearly silly but captivating." "This book about eggs is filled with colorful illustrations and is best for readers who like to think about what they read." "This is a new magazine our library just started subscribing to, and each issue contains several quality literary stories that may be a little hard to read." "Here is a new book of poems by Jack Prelutsky. All of you who loved *The New Kid on the Block* should like this one equally well." "And this is an easy-to-read adventure book about two friends, a mad scientist, and a disappearing corpse." Then get out of the way as students rush to check out shared materials.

To acquaint students with a variety of material in a short time, seat students in a circle and distribute one piece of material to each one, making sure there is a variety of kinds of materials as well as varied reading levels. For one minute, students look over or read their material. Then the teacher calls "Pass" and materials are passed to the student on the left. This routine continues for a set period of time or until students have their original book back. A guaranteed problem: Some students will want to keep a captivating book and not pass it on! Ah, the delights of such "problems."

A teacher book talk is a more formal and organized presentation than sharing. In a book talk, the teacher chooses a book unknown to most students, tells the book's genre, describes the main character in a few words, hints at the plot or theme of the book, possibly reads a brief passage, shows an illustration or two, compares it with a book likely to be known by students, and tells its approximate level of difficulty—all while holding up the book. Because a book talk is brief— probably only about two minutes long—it is best to give more than one at a time.

R. R. Bowker Publishing (245 W. 17th St., NY, NY 10011) publishes two books of ready-made teacher book talks:

> *Primaryplots: A Book Talk Guide for Use with*
> *Readers Ages 4–8.* 1989.
> *Introducing Bookplots: A Book Talk Guide for Use*
> *with Readers Ages 8–12.* 1988.

A variation of a book talk is for the teacher to read a teaser—a paragraph or a page of high interest—but stop in the middle of a sentence or just when something exciting is about to happen. With picture books for younger children, share a few illustrations that pique curiosity but don't reveal the ending. Because of their brevity, share a couple of teasers at a time—and then avoid the stampede that follows when you lay down the materials.

School libraries have library media and audio- and videocassettes on books, authors, and stimulating topics, which fit in well with author/topic studies discussed later in this section. Movies and television shows are another source of stimulation. A few young people's books have been made into movies and these can be shown either to arouse interest in the book or to compare the two media after the teacher has read the book aloud. Books based on television shows are available, and they appeal to many students. A major problem with many of these is that students want the books immediately, when the television show is at its peak, and school libraries can't acquire them that rapidly. (Also, many librarians are understandably reluctant to spend money on books that are obviously a passing fad.)

INTERACTING WITH LESS ABLE READERS

Less able readers and apathetic/reluctant readers are two groups needing the most teacher attention in an independent reading program. We've already discussed helping these students select interesting materials at the appropriate level of difficulty. But these students need more than just appropriate materials; they need a lot of personal attention from the teacher.

An effective way of showing interest and support is to sit with such students during SSR to help them with unrecognized words and to help them stay on task. And even though hard-line proponents of SSR state that the teacher should read along with students during SSR, teachers need to consider the needs of their students. Reading materials students have selected may far outweigh the importance of the teacher reading silently during SSR.

Good readers will read anything, anywhere, anytime. But less able readers need a more conducive environment. One way to create this is to let a reluctant reader choose a classmate with whom to read and where in the room he or she wants to read—coat closet, refrigerator box, reading corner—as long as established rules of behavior are followed.

Nationwide, about 80 percent of the less able readers are boys. As these boys get older, their interest in school reading wanes even though their interest in nonacademic reading grows. These boys will eagerly read comic books and magazines about hot rods, sports, martial arts, and video games; they will lose themselves in catalogs about scientific equipment, guns, sporting goods, and toys; and they will have fun reading the captions of coloring books and announcements on the backs of cereal boxes. With nonacademic material, on-task behavior suddenly is no problem.

Most books and even magazine articles overwhelm these readers with words, words, words. They are too long for the students to complete in a reasonable time, even if they had the reading stamina to do so, which they don't. One answer is minibooks: stories from older basal readers and articles from magazines, stapled inside oak-tag covers decorated by the students. Once stories are removed from hardcover basal readers, there are no grade-level designations and less able readers will avidly read stories from below-grade-level basals—provided the stories are of interest to them. These stories and articles can qualify as "books" for recording, sharing, and reporting purposes. These books can even be used with reading buddies as described on page 61. Some teachers give these books to students for their home library when they have been read. Over a period of time, a teacher, particularly with the help of an aide, can create a sizeable library of minibooks.

Encouraging less able readers to read independently requires more teacher effort and commitment than getting better readers to read. But these are precisely the students who most need personal help and attention.

BULLETIN BOARDS

Bulletin boards can contribute in many ways to a quality independent reading program. There are two kinds of bulletin boards: informative and interactive.

Informative bulletin boards are essentially static displays that can inspire, encourage, and motivate as well as inform. But they are unchanging; what you put up is what you take down. Informative bulletin boards are especially good for acquainting students with books via displays of book jackets. A bulletin board could concentrate on new books, examples of a genre, an author or authors, a topic such as pioneers, or a theme such as friendship. An example is shown below.

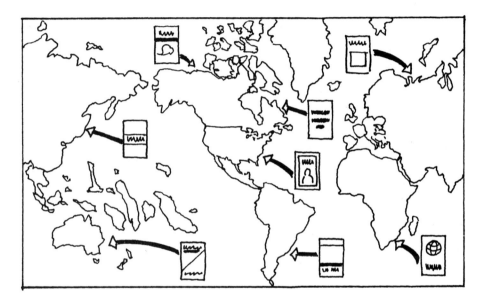

Teachers can whet students' appetite for reading the book by adding catchy phrases under the jacket such as "Huge dog causes humorous problems for owners," "Ancient curse brings evil and death," or "Would Tyrannosaurs have made good pets?"

Many teachers either encourage or require students to read at least one book from several different categories—e.g., biography, animals, other countries, historical fiction. A bulletin board could show the categories chosen for such a requirement and appropriate book jackets could be displayed in each selected category.

Good informative bulletin boards can do more than display book jackets. A list of creative ways that students could share their reading (see "Student Sharing of and Creatively Reacting to Books," pages 42–45) or various ways students could report on what they've read (see "Reports," pages 45–51) is also appropriate for informative bulletin boards.

Interactive bulletin boards get students more involved than informative ones. Most of the ideas listed in "Reporting" can be converted into a bulletin board. Students love writing the name of a completed book (and possibly their name) on a construction-paper ice-cream scoop and adding it to a bulletin-board cone (See at right.) Gravity-defying curves and loops merely add to the pleasure.

Interactive bulletin boards let students share their reading with others. Brief reports containing a summary of the book and the reader's evaluation of it can be posted on an appropriately titled bulletin board and entice other students to read the reports. (See below.)

There are many books of reading-bulletin-board ideas available from school-supply stores and college libraries. School librarians usually have several of them. The magazines *Instructor*, *Teacher*, *Learning*, and *Teaching K–8* regularly publish bulletin-board ideas. Check current and back issues.

Here are some guidelines regarding bulletin boards:

1. The more you involve students, the more likely the goals of the bulletin board will be attained than if you do all the work yourself. If students choose and hang the book jackets, cut and attach the ice-cream scoops, select the categories for required reading, or even decide the topic of a bulletin board—a football game, hot-air balloons, bubblegum balls in a dispenser—the bulletin board will be more meaningful to them. And let them remove it when you're through with it. Even informative bulletin boards can become interactive to some degree.

2. A bulletin board can be time-consuming to construct and incredibly short-lived. The topics chosen and the time required to construct it should be commensurate with its values. Colorful borders, cutout letters, laminating, and illustrations can demand an inordinate amount of time that could be better spent acquainting yourself with new books in the school library.

3. Avoid bulletin boards that encourage competition among students.

4. Plan so that the bulletin board can be redisplayed in the future. Make parts small enough to store flat in a manila envelope or a file folder. For example, rather than one large sheet showing the islands of Japan, display each of the main islands separately.

5. Use the bulletin board in some way; don't just construct an aesthetic space filler. Point it out to students: discuss it; periodically call their attention to it.

AUTHOR/TOPIC STUDY
Exploring authors and topics in depth can stimulate independent reading as well as expand and deepen knowledge of authors and topics. Sometimes two birds can be killed with one stone.

In an *author study*, the teacher chooses an author of

several books at the students' reading and interest level. There are several ways the study itself can be conducted. One way is for each student to have a copy of the same paperback book by the selected author and for the teacher to guide the students through the book, chapter by chapter, with appropriate pre- and post—reading activities. This would be the instructional reading program, not independent reading. As part of this study, the teacher can display the author's books, exhibit a poster about the author, read selected information about the author, read to students parts of one or more books, play available audio- or videotapes of an interview with the author. Students can research the author in the school library and/or check out books by the author and add to the display. The cooperation of the school-library media specialist is crucial for success in author studies.

A recommendation that repeatedly pops up with regard to author studies is for individual students or the whole class to write to an author. Even though this may sound appealing, give it some thought. Do students expect the author to respond personally? And by when? How realistic is this considering the tens of thousands of classrooms there are and the handful of popular authors? Don't set the students up for a disappointment; the Berensteins and Beverly Cleary may be too busy to write. And some authors may be very difficult or impossible to contact.

A *topic study* is conducted in much the same way as is an author study. It can be a topic being studied in a curricular area (whales, electricity, Brazil), a teacher-selected topic based on known student interests, or even a student-selected topic. Some teachers have a different topic each month and even require students to read at least one book or article on the topic to assure that they read something other than fiction. Individual students or small groups may select an appropriate subtopic, create a display of objects and reading materials, and share it with the class.

Sources for ideas for topic studies besides those from curricular areas are ideas in monthly calendars of *Instructor*, *Learning*, and *Teaching K–8*. Besides the obvious holidays and events, there are some highly relevant ones most of us might not be aware of—e.g., Pet Week, National School Lunch Week, National 4-H Week, National Jogging Month, National Hispanic Heritage Month, International Friendship Month, Native American Day, and Black History Month. Inspirational birthdays and anniversaries are also listed, such as the death of the last passenger pigeon, Mayflower Day, Lewis Carroll's birthday, Wright Brothers Day, and Hiroshima Day, .

Both the author and topic study lend themselves to a variety of related activities such as original writing, art projects, oral reports, media and videotape presentations, talks by resource persons, and even creative dramatics. Specially designed ways of recording, sharing, and reporting independent reading can be correlated with the author or topic and used during this period of study, as can bulletin boards and other displays. Related ideas are described in "Reading Corner," page 24.

Where does independent reading fit into all of this? Simple. The more books, authors, and printed materials students are exposed to, the more their interests expand, the more self-motivating they become with regard to reading, and the more positive their attitudes toward reading become. And the easier it is for the teacher to conduct an independent reading program.

READING BUDDIES

We're all social animals and doing something with somebody is more fun than doing it alone. Pair a reluctant reader with another student—particularly a younger one—and presto, instant readers! Having one student read aloud to another is a simple and effective way to stimulate independent reading. There are countless variations on this technique, but they all follow this outline:

1. Pairs can either be students' choices or assigned by the teacher. Pairings are temporary and are rotated regularly. Students may be paired on reading level, reading interests, friendship, or at random. As long as partners are changed regularly, the basis for pairing doesn't seem to make much difference.

2. Pairs can be approximately the same reading level and take turns reading aloud from supplementary basal readers or a paperback novel while the other follows along silently in his or her own copy.

3. Each student can have a different book and they can alternate reading aloud to each other. (The first time a teacher told me about her second-semester first graders using this procedure, I thought, *How confusing; how nonsensical.* But after observing for just a couple of minutes, I changed my mind.)

4. Older students can read to and listen to younger students read. This can be very effective with less-skilled upper-grade readers, because with approval and without stigma, they read materials closer to their reading level than their grade-level instructional reading materials. The upper-grade students can either prepare materials in advance or read material selected by the younger student. Reading the material more than once—at least once in preparation and then once to the younger student—helps sight words become more automatic and reading more fluent.

5. Groups of three and four can be just as successful—although somewhat more difficult to manage. A schedule can be established, and the designated reader(s) can even have selected and practiced on some special material or just read aloud parts of their independent reading books.

6. Younger students can even read to a favorite doll or a teddy bear. One first-grade teacher cut life-size dolls from brown paper, let the students draw clothes and facial features with crayons and felt-tip pens, stuffed them with newspaper, stapled around the edge, and created instant "reading buddies" that the first graders read to with delight and gusto.

Reading buddies can be scheduled weekly or a couple times per month. It can be either a whole-class activity or with selected students. Teachers have even extended this procedure beyond school so that after school, on weekends, or in the summer, students read to shut-ins, patients in nursing homes, the blind, or "adopted grandparents."

Obviously one key to success if done with another class is careful planning with the other teacher.

HOME AND SCHOOL

The student's home can be a potent and positive ally in an independent reading program, and teachers and the school should be ready and willing to take advantage of its potential. Many teachers send general notes to students' homes about their reading programs. (See page 65.)

The most obvious possibility is for students to take independent reading books home and read them silently or aloud or share them with family members. If schoolbooks go home, a teacher may need an efficient checkout and return system, particularly in kindergarten and first grade, where students may not be as responsible as older students in returning books. One recommendation is a chart hung somewhere in the room containing a library envelope for each student. A checkout card can be placed in the envelope at the end of the day where it will be easily seen the next morning, indicating whether the book has been returned.

If teachers require independent reading, forms parents can sign to verify home reading have already been discussed in "Recording."

It is sometimes suggested that family members discuss the book with the child or even have the child retell the story to someone. But not all educators agree that this is a proper home function with regard to independent reading. Some believe that the home should only provide the time and place for independent reading but shouldn't take the place of the teacher. They fear that discussing or retelling the story can easily make independent reading a chore and not a pleasure, particularly with parents who may not know how to discuss their child's reading without causing tension and anxiety—two no-nos of independent reading. A caveat: don't impulsively urge parents to discuss their child's home reading with the child.

Teachers and schools have inaugurated organized read-at-home programs such as the one described in the following pages. Teachers need to assess home schedules and determine whether two, three, four, or five weekly periods are most realistic and how long each one should be: 10, 15, or 20 minutes.

The contract on page 66 is worth examining. Four parties sign a pledge to work together to create a successful independent reading program. Such a solemn action, if done sincerely, binds all four in a union to reach a common goal. Surely a noble endeavor.

As noted previously, modifications such as substituting number of minutes or number of pages for number of books is possible.

Some teachers have found plastic bags handy for sending books home, particularly if an audiocassette accompanies the book.

A book swap can energize student independent reading and promote home-school cooperation. A note is sent home inviting students to bring good used books they want to trade. A form signed by the parents with the name(s) of the book(s) to be traded is brought to school along with the books. An exchange coupon is given for each paperback book in good condition, with hardback or larger books being worth two coupons. Books are marked showing the number of coupons each is worth. Students are permitted to browse through the books for a day or two before trading day. A schedule permits one student at a time to select one book. The rotation continues until all the books have been selected. Swapped books may be read immediately, taken home to be read, or read during SSR on subsequent school days.

Useful brochures about the role of the home in children's reading development are available from several educational organizations and publishers of instructional reading material. Teachers should ask publishers' representatives whether their company has any of these. Often they are free or cost very little. The International Reading Association (800 Barksdale

COLORADO SCHOOL

TO: Parents of Colorado School's 2nd and 3rd Graders
FROM: Principal
TOPIC: The Improvement of Your Child's Reading

This is a reading enrichment program designed to involve parents in their children's learning.

In the majority of homes, more time is spent watching TV than reading. We are proposing a "READING ENRICHES ALL CHILDREN'S HOMES" (REACH) program that will encourage more reading by lessening the amount of time spent watching television. Parents want to be involved in their children's learning and all that is needed is for the school to provide meaningful ways in which parents can contribute.

In the REACH program, parents of second- and third-grade children are asked to sign a contract with the school saying that the TV will be turned off for at least one-half (1/2) hour two evenings a week to allow time for reading. We encourage each family member to have some type of material to read at this time. The school is encouraging the use of our elementary library or public library.

When ten books have been read and verified by the parent, the student will be given a certificate which will be presented at an assembly program each month or as needed. After 50 books, a book award will be given. Classroom teachers will monitor the program and identify award recipients.

After you have read the enclosed program materials, if you have any questions, please call me. Your cooperation and support will make the project a success. Without it, we cannot hope to succeed.

Thank you for helping.

READING ENRICHES ALL CHILDREN'S HOMES
(REACH)
Parents and Children Enjoying Reading

CONTRACT

Student: I, _____ , agree to read at least ten (10) books during our family reading time.

Parent: I, _____ , agree to arrange a family reading time of at least fifteen (15) minutes twice a week when we will turn off our TV and enjoy reading together. I will notify my child's teacher whenever the child completes ten (10) books at home.

Teacher: I, _____ , will encourage my students to fulfill their contacts. I will keep records of the books read and notify the principal when students are eligible for awards.

Principal: I, _____ , will present a certificate to each student who reads ten books at home. After fifty books, a book award will be given. The presentation will be made at an assembly program for all REACH participants.

This contract becomes binding when all four responsible parties have signed in the above blanks.

Date this contract was signed: _____

Date this contract is to be completed: _____

Road, P.O. Box 8139, Newark, DE 19714-8139) publishes inexpensive brochures for parents. Some titles are:

Good Books Make Reading Fun for Your Child
Summer Reading Is Important
You Can Encourage Your Child to Read
*You Can Help Your Child in Reading by Using the
    Newspaper*
Your Home Is Your Child's First School

Some of these brochures are available in French and Spanish as well as English. Prices can be obtained by writing the IRA at the above address.

As helpful as these brochures are, they shouldn't merely be sent home with students or given to parents without any explanation. They are primarily supplements to a larger program. Parents who could benefit most from such brochures will need a low-key, tactful, positive message from the teacher. But even after brochures are distributed in such a fashion, teachers shouldn't delude themselves that miracles will occur and the children in these families will avidly embrace independent reading. Such brochures are only one course, not the whole banquet.

Part of a good home-school program is making sure students have a local public-library card. Teachers should take their class to the local public library, acquaint them with how to use it, and have the students check out a book or two to take home. These teachers also encourage parents to apply for a library card if they don't have one and to make regular trips to the public library with their children. Books checked out from the public library can be read during SSR time and counted toward meeting any reading requirements.

Summer presents a challenge for teachers who value independent reading programs. The best programs continue in some way over the summer. Some possibilities include:

1. Communicate with parents about the summer reading program at the local public library, the bookmobile, or local school libraries.

2. Take your students to the public library near the end of the school year and send home checked-out books along with information about the summer reading program.

3. Near the end of school, have students complete a list of three to ten books they'd like to read during the summer. Send the list to parents with an accompanying letter.

4. Send home a list of some of the most popular books read in class in the past year and encourage parents to check out from the public library any their child might want to read.

5. With old April or May issues of *Instructor, Learning*, or *Teaching K–8*, compile a list of books recommended for summer reading.

6. During the summer, send one or more letters to students and parents encouraging reading and visits to the public library or the local school library if it's open. You might want to recommend titles to read aloud or read alone.

THE READING-WRITING-READING CONNECTION
Independent reading programs needn't include only materials written by adults for students. What students write for each other will be avidly read by classmates and younger students. When students' writing—fiction and nonfiction—has been edited and rewritten, covers can be made with the pages stapled inside them. These books can be part of the classroom or the central school library. And because students tend to write one to three grade levels below their grade placement, such books are quite suitable for younger students, particularly in a reading buddy program such as the one described earlier.

The finished product can be as elaborate as teacher and student time and desire permit. Illustrations can be drawn, covers decorated, and even checkout cards created and inserted in a glued-in pocket inside the back cover.

Authors can read their own compositions to others. They can read works-in-progress to a classmate or two or finished student books to the whole class or to younger reading buddies.

New teachers shouldn't unthinkingly embark upon such a project. Orchestrating the whole activity can be difficult. Writing a book requires a considerable amount of time; composing a coherent story demands student and teacher perseverance and considerable editing and rewriting, and not all students can produce a readable composition. But when finished, even mediocre as well as excellent student books produce nearly magical responses from other students. "These are the most frequently read books in the classroom," one teacher commented.

Cooperative Celebrations

"The more the merrier" applies to stimulating independent reading as well as to social gatherings. Even though many of the activities described so far could be extended to incorporate more than one teacher, most of them have focused on the individual teacher and his or her students. This section describes several celebrations involving more than one teacher: a book fair, a National Library Week celebration, and a Friday-night sleep-over.

BOOK FAIR

A book fair is for the whole family. Books and magazines are available to buy or swap; there are games and activities related to books, and possibly an author of children's books to discuss his or her publications. A book fair can be any size you are capable of managing. With parental and community help, it can involve a whole school.

Books for exhibit and sale can come from publishers, state departments of education, and professional organizations such as the Children's Book Council. The school-library media specialist has or can get this information.

Even student-written books can be part of the display.

In a book swap, students bring hardback and paperback books to a central school location and receive tickets indicating the number and quality of books brought in. During the book fair, students can exchange these tickets for books donated by other students.

Before the fair, students can design posters, bookmarks, book jackets, mobiles, and bulletin boards, write creative book reports, and set up displays of classroom libraries—all of which can be on show before and during the fair.
At the fair, activities such as the following can be arranged:

1. Book quizzes. Book jackets without titles can be displayed, and students can write titles. The student or class with the most correct answers wins a prize. Characters, settings, or plots could substitute for book jackets. There is even computer software containing questions about popular best-selling children's books that could be used.

2. Parade of students dressed as book characters.

3. Puppet shows and flannel-board stories based on books.

4. Filmstrips and videotapes about books and authors can be shown.

5. Episodes from books can be dramatized by groups of students.

Free printed information for parents can be distributed. Some possible materials were described in the section "Home and School," page 64. Also, a sheet listing books for sale with a blank space for writing titles to be bought or read should be furnished.

Successful book fairs require several committees and much planning. But because of the interest in independent reading they can generate, educators find them worthwhile.

A NATIONAL LIBRARY WEEK CELEBRATION
Weeklong celebrations involving several teachers or a whole school can focus attention on books and stimulate interest in reading more powerfully than the efforts of an individual teacher. Following is a brief description of what one school did.

Monday	Bookmark Day. Students made original bookmarks featuring aspects of favorite books or a slogan about books or reading. In addition, each child was given a printed bookmark encouraging family members to read aloud at the dinner table every evening.
Tuesday	Read-Alert Day. Three times during the day the school principal announced over the intercom, "Stop everything and read something." Students and staff carried selected reading materials with them at all times.
Wednesday	Library Volunteer Recognition Day. Each adult and student volunteer received a flower, and donated books were added to the school library, one to recognize the contributions of each volunteer. A "Paddington Bear" play was presented at this program by a group of sixth graders for students in kindergarten through third grade.
Thursday	Door Poster Day. Each class selected a favorite book and created a colorful door-size poster about it featuring the title and author, characters, and scenes. The art teacher helped with layout, materials, and painting. These were displayed on the outside of classroom doors so students walking the hall could see them.
Friday	Book Character Day. All students were asked to wear something that would identify them as a character from a book they enjoyed. (A simple placard could substitute for a full costume.)

During the week, each grade had a special speaker or resource visit. A great-grandmother of one of the teachers told kindergartners a folktale, and the school-library media specialist involved first graders in a play about the book *Caps for Sale*. A folk singer sang for fourth through sixth graders and shared books about the people in his songs. The district media director showed second graders slides of famous children's authors she had met whose books were in the school library. A library media specialist from another school, a specialist on Laura Ingalls Wilder, made a presentation to third graders on the *Little House* books. A professional football player who had student-taught in the school talked with fourth graders about sports books. The school superintendent read to fifth graders a favorite book from his childhood, and the editor of the local newspaper talked about his favorite books and what books had meant to him.

Teachers could adapt this model to their own situation, creating activities appropriate for them and their students—and sustaining interest in independent reading over an entire week.

FRIDAY NIGHT SLEEP-OVER

Ideally a sleep-over begins at 7:00 p.m. on Friday and ends on Saturday at 8:00 a.m. Each student brings a sleeping bag, pillow, stuffed animal—and lots of reading materials. The schedule alternates 30-minute blocks of reading with 30-minute group activities such as aerobics, singing, viewing a movie or a puppet show, or listening to a story.

In the morning, volunteers prepare breakfast, the principal announces the total number of pages read, and award certificates are distributed to all participants.

A modified program can end at 10:30 or 11:00 p.m. with no sleep-over.

A sleep-over can provide as much SSR in one evening—as much as 150 minutes—as most students can get in two to three weeks of school.

The complexity of organizing and operating such a venture should not be underestimated. Volunteers must be recruited and oriented, teachers and students prepared, activities scheduled, parents informed, equipment gathered, and numerous details planned. The School Division of D. C. Heath and Company (125 Spring St., Lexington, MA 02173) has published a resource guide, *Friday Night Prime Time*, describing sleep-over activities and listing the tasks and responsibilities.

TO SUM UP

The three cooperative celebrations described in this section are merely illustrative, not exhaustive. Other possibilities exist or can be created. Ambitious educators can create ones appropriate for their own situations and resources. Cooperative celebrations needn't be grandiose affairs; they can be scaled to available resources.

Their primary value is that they unmistakably announce to students and parents that independent reading is so important that a group of teachers or the whole school will make it the focus for an extended period of time, that independent reading isn't just a bit of fluff attended to when there are a few extra minutes at the end of the day. On the contrary, it is so valued that for a period of time, other curricular activities take a backseat to it. "Where your time is, there shall your values be seen."

Teacher-Suggested Guidelines for Creating a Program

An independent reading program is more than regular periods of SSR and an occasional sharing of books by teacher and students. It is planned and organized. It considers the whole curriculum, including instructional reading. The teachers who submitted the ideas in this book suggested the following guidelines, particularly for inexperienced or novice teachers.

1. Keep the whole reading program—instructional and independent—in perspective. Too much time devoted to reading creates an unbalanced school curriculum. Some students can be more stimulated to read independently by a good science lesson than by 15 minutes of being read to by a teacher.

2. Keep the instructional reading program in perspective. Four days of reading instruction per week may be very adequate in most classrooms, and in some of them, three days a week will be enough. Some or all of the remaining day(s) can be used for independent reading activities.

3. Plan the *instructional reading program* to take advantage of variety in core instructional materials, appropriate but not excessive skill instruction, varied grouping arrangements, and stimulating extended and enrichment activities as suggested earlier in "The Foundation of a Quality Independent Reading Program," pages 11–13. To help do this, a blank skeleton form is shown on page 78.

4. Keep the *independent reading program* in perspective. A quality independent reading program includes teacher oral reading and student sharing in addition to SSR, library visits, creative reporting, teacher book talks, and various other activities. Because they are so enjoyable and stimulating for both teacher and students, it's easy to devote an excessive amount of time to them. A blank form for planning the independent reading program for a nine-week period is shown on page 80. Use the monthly calendars referred to in "Author/Topic Study," pages 59-61, to help identify special days and weeks.

5. Plan a small-scale, low-key project for the first week, e.g., initiate SSR and have students make individual reading folders. Wait until later in the year—when you have adequate classroom control—to schedule large-scale projects.

6. Select activities by skimming the suggestions in this book and choosing one or two you can implement at the beginning of the year with a minimum of planning. Discuss them with the class before beginning. So often students have excellent ideas or insights that will make the activity more successful.

7. When you look over the suggestions in this book, be open-minded. Ask yourself, How can I modify them to best suit my situation? Is this likely to promote too much competition? Can all students participate equally? How long should it last? Could I do it with help? If so, who would help?

8. Get input from others before embarking on a large-scale, long-term, complicated project. Talk with other teachers, the media-center director, the principal—possibly even the custodian. (Don't just assume you can tape footprints to the corridor walls!) Also, coordinate it with neighboring teachers so there's no interference with their projects.

9. Evaluate the value and soundness of a large-scale project. One teacher carried out the following project:

> After reading a paperback novel, the students worked in groups of two or three and either depicted a passage from their book by painting a poster for background scenery or by constructing dioramas or models. If appropriate, they also dressed like the characters. The teacher then took photographs of their scenes and had prints made which were given to each student. At Open House, she showed the slide show to parents.

Before embarking on such projects, evaluate them by asking what goals they will achieve, how much teacher and student time they will take, what will they cost, and whether they are worth it. Size and scope don't necessarily translate into sound educational practices.

10. Be judicious about competition and about giving out prizes and rewards. A teacher recommended giving students a brown paper bag to decorate. These were hung on a bulletin board. Each time a student wrote a book report about books read, a line two inches up from the bottom was marked on the bag. After a predetermined length of time, there was a popcorn party and students got to fill their bags according to the line on their bag. Students could fill more than one bag.

How necessary is a toy, a candy bar, a personal pizza, a McDonald's coupon? Could such incentives give students an incorrect motivation for reading? ("What will you give me if I read ten books?")

11. Use the form on page 80 to assess your independent reading program.

THE INSTRUCTIONAL READING PROGRAM: A LONG RANGE PLAN

Week	Core Instructional Material	Supplemental Material	Skills to Emphasize	Extended/ Enrichment Activities	Grouping Arrangement(s)

THE INDEPENDENT READING PROGRAM
A LONG-RANGE PLAN

Week	Teacher Oral Reading	Special Day(s); Week	Activities/Projects
1			1) Initiate SSR. 2) Personal reading folders.
2			
3			
4			
5			
6			
7			
8			
9			

Book Week is mid-November.
National Library Week is early April.
Your school librarian will have information. Should you want
to contact the sponsoring organization, write to:

Children's Book council (Book Week)
67 Irving Place
New York, NY 10003

American Library Association (National Library Week)
50 East Huron
Chicago, IL 60611

AN IDEAL
INDEPENDENT-READING PROGRAM:
A CHECKLIST

	Needs Improvement	Adequate	Excellent
1. Varied and appropriate reading material	1	2	3
2. Teacher oral reading	1	2	3
3. Teacher sharing of materials	1	2	3
4. Individual teacher-student conferences	1	2	3
5. Displays (bulletin boards, posters, mobiles)	1	2	3
6. Reading corner	1	2	3
7. Students' reading interests determined and used	1	2	3
8. Students independently select appropriate-level materials	1	2	3
9. Sustained silent reading (SSR) time	1	2	3
10. Motivational records of independent reading	1	2	3
11. Student competition minimized	1	2	3
12. Student sharing of and creative reacting to books	1	2	3
13. Creative oral and written reporting	1	2	3
14. Special attention to less-able readers	1	2	3
15. Author and/or topic study	1	2	3
16. Reading buddies	1	2	3
17. Home-school cooperation	1	2	3
18. Reading-writing-reading connection	1	2	3
19. Cooperative celebrations	1	2	3
20. Long-range planning	1	2	3